Sing, Aretha, Sing!

ARETHA FRANKLIN,
"Respect," and the Civil Rights Movement

Hanif Abdurraqib   Illustrated by Ashley Evans

FARRAR STRAUS GIROUX

New York

The Queen of Soul first sang gospel in the old southern churches, and her songs shook the walls. She sang in the church and people spilled out of their pews and into the aisles, and the people would shout, *Sing, Aretha, sing!* and sway in each other's arms.

When Aretha sang, the clouds would puff themselves wide and break away from the sun, and the sun would smile down on the faces of the children who stopped their games in the street when Aretha sang.

Aretha left her father's church when she was sixteen years old to go on tour across the United States with Dr. Martin Luther King Jr.

She sang while he preached to people about
the coming civil rights movement and how all
people deserved to be treated as equals.
And while she sang, and while he preached,
Aretha saw people getting a little more
free than they were.

And when Aretha started making records in the 1950s, she sang to uplift her people first. She sang about love and freedom and survival.

One day in 1967, when Aretha was twenty-four,
she sat down at a piano in New York and sang a song.

R-E-S-P-E-C-T
sang Aretha.

Find out what it means to me!
sang Aretha.

And out of Aretha's mouth came a soulful sound,
and on the streets of New York, people shouted,
Sing, Aretha, sing! and pumped their fists to the sky.

The summer of 1967 grew hot. The sun ran behind the clouds, which puffed out their dark gray cheeks and shook waves of water from their bodies. On the streets below, people marched and raised their voices against war and racism, and buildings in cities caught fire.

Waves of joy and singing in the streets were replaced with walls of blue police officers pushing down on the Black people who wanted to dance and love where they pleased, and people were standing up for their rights.

And Aretha, who once sang for Dr. Martin Luther King Jr., said, *I see you, Black and fighting for a country to love you.*

Aretha sang **R-E-S-P-E-C-T** and spelled out the word nice and long two times so that the people would have something to hang on to. And each letter of the word drifted by—

R and the rustling branches of the trees awoke

E and the early-morning protests swelled

S and the summer swayed

P and the puddles of water from the rain were splashed in

E and the eager church walls shook

C and the clouds pulled away from the sun

T and two hands linked and then two more and the people
could not be moved, and the song became an
anthem for the civil rights movement.

People sang it on long and hot marches.
People sang it with fists and batons crashing
down on their bodies.

Black people picked their afros high and danced to the song in
basements, or at parties, or when it played out of stereos at night.
The song lifted their bodies up and puffed them as wide as the
clouds, and it gave them new power when they felt like they hadn't
had it for so long.

Aretha played "Respect" in front of people in cities far and wide, and the song told those people, *You can take back what is yours.*

The song echoed in the spirit of everything Aretha learned in the church and in the spirit of everything Aretha learned singing with Dr. Martin Luther King Jr. How sometimes the right words and the right sound could open a window and let a small bit of freedom through.

And the fight for civil rights didn't end with "Respect," but now there was a song for the struggle. A song can make the people come together with one voice and sing. And this was another type of freedom, to have joy while a world outside was trying to take it away.

Aretha sang about **RESPECT** and the world moved.
Aretha sang about **RESPECT** and the people demanded **RESPECT**.
A song cannot change the world by itself, but it can be the wings that
fly from the mouths of the people wanting to change the world.

Today, **RESPECT** is still in the wind, echoing from generation down to generation, and maybe there is a song in you waiting to spill out and make the world a better place to dance in and love in and start a revolution in.

The streets are waiting to be met with the rhythm, and the wind is waiting to curve around the words of your anthem, and carried with the wind will be Aretha, always humming

R-E-S-P-E-C-T

Author's Note

Because of the size and scope of this book, only so much of Aretha Franklin's life could be honored. I wanted, of course, to give ample space to Aretha the singer, and Aretha who grew up singing in churches. But it also felt important to offer small parts of a fuller picture. I think Black artists sometimes do not get to be more than the one thing they're known for. Or, their legacies are tied most intensely to their output.

Beyond her singing, Aretha Franklin was an artist who worked to serve other artists. She was mentored by the great gospel singer Clara Ward, and Aretha paid that mentoring forward throughout her career. She was a generous duet partner to musicians through all generations—everyone from a young Brandy in the '90s, to the legendary Big Mama Thornton, near the end of her long life in the '80s.

I also wanted to offer a look at Aretha Franklin as a political figure, and I did not want her political engagement to be lost in her legacy as a one-of-a-kind singer. For much of Aretha's life, she prioritized the civil rights struggle, and the struggle for women's rights. In 1970, she gave an interview in *Jet* magazine in support of activist Angela Davis, who was jailed at the time. Aretha insisted in the interview that Davis must be freed because, as she put it, "She's a Black woman who wants freedom for Black people."

Her songs, like "Respect," became anthems for civil rights and women's rights movements, and Aretha often performed at protests throughout the '60s and '70s. (While the song "Respect" was actually first written and recorded by soul singer Otis Redding in 1965, Aretha's 1967 version is the most well known.) She provided money for civil rights groups and bailed out activists. She fought on the behalf of marginalized people, no matter where she was in her career. In the 1960s, Aretha put a clause in her contract stating that she would not sing in front of segregated audiences. She was unafraid to risk the power she'd earned and attained through an admiration for her work. She learned and gained an affection for the Civil Rights Movement, in part, through Dr. Martin Luther King Jr., who was a frequent guest in Aretha's home when she was young, connecting with her father. When Aretha was sixteen, she went on gospel tours with King, and along the way, helped form the politics that would propel her through decades of singing, and decades of living.

When Aretha died in 2018, her funeral service was long. It was a nearly all-day affair, with people from various backgrounds coming to speak about how she had touched their lives. There were gospel singers, but also pop singers, but also civil rights leaders, but also athletes, and so on. That wide variety of folks ready and willing to speak to Aretha's impact defined what I believe her reach to be. And not just her musical reach, either—but also her very genuine ability to save parts of herself for her people, and the many fights that they were immersed in.

After witnessing the funeral, I knew that I wanted to invest myself in this book, with the hopes that there could be another generation who found their way to Aretha Franklin's life and history in a way that lived beyond her albums. When I was growing up, I heard songs and found my way to a great many musicians just off the strength of their music alone. But it was less common for me to hear about the musicians themselves, or the stories of their lives. The hope is that this book provides some context for the fullness of Aretha Franklin. And that, in doing so, a new generation of Aretha fans emerge and pass the music on to those they love. So that her legacy can flourish well beyond these decades.

For Aretha. —H.A.

For my mom.
Thank you for nurturing the song in my heart
and giving me the love of music and art. —A.E.

Farrar Straus Giroux Books for Young Readers
An imprint of Macmillan Publishing Group, LLC
120 Broadway, New York, NY 10271 • mackids.com

Library of Congress Cataloging-in-Publication Data
Names: Abdurraqib, Hanif, 1983– author. I Evans, Ashley, illustrator.
Title: Sing, Aretha, sing! : Aretha Franklin, "Respect," and the civil rights movement / Hanif Abdurraqib ; pictures by Ashley Evans.
Description: New York : Farrar Straus Giroux Books for Young Readers, 2021. I Audience: Grades 2–3 I Summary: "An empowering picture book biography
of Aretha Franklin and her role in civil rights, perfect for Women's History Month and Black History Month" —Provided by publisher.
Identifiers: LCCN 2021027782 I ISBN 9780374313456 (hardcover)
Subjects: LCSH: Franklin, Aretha—Juvenile literature. I Soul musicians—United States—Biography. I African American singers—Biography—Juvenile
literature. I Singers—United States—Biography—Juvenile literature. I Civil rights movements—United States—20th century—Juvenile literature.
Classification: LCC ML3930.F68 A23 2021 I DDC 782.421644092 [B]—dc23
LC record available at https://lccn.loc.gov/2021027782

First edition, 2021 • Book design by Sharismar Rodriguez
The art was created digitally, using Procreate and Photoshop.
Printed in China by Hung Hing Off-set Printing Co. Ltd., Heshan City, Guangdong Province

ISBN 978-0-374-31345-6 (hardcover)
1 3 5 7 9 10 8 6 4 2